TransIt-TIGER
Authoring
Shell

●●●●●●●●●●●●●●●●

Technology Enhanced Language Learning

Hodder & Stoughton

A MEMBER OF THE HODDER HEADLINE GROUP

ACKNOWLEDGEMENTS

DESIGN/PEDAGOGY

D Thompson, J Thompson, University of Hull; P J Corness,
F H Deepwell, Coventry University.

PROGRAMMING

C R Daniels, Coventry University

Toolbook is a Trademark of Asymetrix Corporation
Windows is a Trademark of Microsoft Corporation

About TELL

TELL stands for Technology Enhanced Language Learning. The TELL series of courseware products has been conceived and produced as part of the TLTP – the Teaching and Learning Technology Programme – a major initiative funded by the Higher Education Funding bodies for England, Scotland, Wales and Northern Ireland. TELL courseware has been created by a consortium of universities and other higher education institutions, led by the CTI Centre for Modern Languages at the University of Hull.

CONTENTS

∙∙∙∙∙∙∙∙∙∙∙∙∙∙∙∙∙∙

Licence

TransIt-TIGER Authoring Shell is subject to copyright law. This licence allows you to use the package on up ot 10 computers within a single institution.

However, if your higher education institution is funded by HEFCE, SHEFC, HEFCW or DENI, and if your institution received this package under the TLTP distribution arrangements, you may make copies of the manuals and disks for use on computers within a single institution, or you may install the package on a network for use within that institution.

In all other cases, if you wish to use the package on more than ten machines you must purchase the appropriate network licence from the TELL Consortium.

Materials produced using the TransIt-TIGER Authoring Shell may not be distributed outside the UK higher education sector and may not be sold commercially.
TransIt-TIGER Authoring Shell contains certain Redistributable Files and Clip Files which are licensed under an *Asymetrix ToolBook* Family Software License Agreement. That agreement includes the following provisions affecting those Files (covered hereinafter by the term "the Software") which extend to any users of *TransIt-TIGER Authoring Shell*:

Hardware requirements
IBM PC or compatible. The TELL Consortium cannot guarantee that this product will run on any network.

Technical support
For technical support, email tell-support@langc.hull.ac.uk For those without access to email, the technical support fax line is +44(0)1482 473816 and the phone line is +44(0)1482 465872

Please ensure that you have to hand the name of the program, its version number and full details of what the problem is before you phone the support line.

First published 1997

ISBN 0 340 66981 0

© The University of Hull 1997

Typeset by GreenGate Publishing Services, Tonbridge, Kent
Printed and bound in Great Britain for Hodder and Stoughton Educational,
a division of Hodder Headline plc, 338 Euston Road, London NW1 3BH, by Circle Services, Southend, Essex.

Installing the TransIt-TIGER Authoring Shell

SYSTEM REQUIREMENTS

To install and use *TransIt-TIGER Authoring Shell* you need:

- an 80386 or higher PC with a 3.5" high density floppy disk drive
- Microsoft Windows 3.1 or higher
- a hard disk with at least 5 MB of free disk space
- a VGA or higher resolution monitor
- at least 4 MB of RAM (8 MB is recommended).

*NB: If you have the development version of **Asymetrix ToolBook** installed on your system you should read the Technical Notes section at the end of this manual, as well as the installation instructions below.*

1 INSTALLATION ON A STAND-ALONE MACHINE
....

1 Start Windows
2 insert the *TransIt-TIGER Authoring Shell* disk 1 in a floppy disk drive
3 in the Program Manager window, select the **File** menu
4 choose the **Run...** option from the **File** menu
5 in the command line box, type

a:\setup

then choose the OK button

6 follow the instructions on screen.

During the installation routine, you are able to create a name for the subdirectory and the path where *TransIt-TIGER Authoring Shell* will be installed. Otherwise, by default, the package is automatically installed in **c:\ttshell** on the hard disk. The routine also creates a *TransIt-TIGER* program group and an icon under the Windows Program Manager, from which you can start up the package.

1.1 Installing the ToolBook runtime to a non-default directory

TransIt-TIGER uses the *Asymetrix ToolBook* runtime modules. Setup will install the runtime by default in the directory **c:\Windows\asym\runtime**, but if you wish to install it to a different directory choose the Custom option in the Setup routine, then choose **Change MMTB runtime directory...** and specify a directory either by typing in the full pathname in the space provided or by using the **Browse** button to choose a directory. If the directory you specify doesn't exist Setup will create it for you.

1.2 Foregoing ToolBook runtime installation

If you have previously installed another version of *TransIt-TIGER* you will already have the *ToolBook* runtime modules on your system and thus will not need to re-install them. To forego installation of the runtime choose the **Custom** option in the Setup routine, then choose **Change MMTB runtime directory...**, and in the resulting dialogue uncheck the **Install MMTB runtime** check box.

For further details regarding the operation of the *ToolBook* runtime, and how *Translt-TIGER* uses previously-installed versions of *ToolBook,* please see the Technical Notes section at the end of this manual.

2 INSTALLATION ON A NETWORK

Network installation should be carried out by a competent Network Manager, adopting the following procedure:

1 run **setup.exe** from *Translt-TIGER Authoring Shell* disk 1 (or copy the files from both install disks to a network drive and run **setup** from there)
2 in Setup specify a destination directory for the *Translt-TIGER* application files
3 specify a destination directory for the *ToolBook* runtime modules (optional: see Section 1.2 above).

Setup will optionally create a program group and application icon. To create an application icon manually use the following command line in the Program Item Properties dialogue:

<runtime dir.>\mtb30run.exe *<application dir.>*\ttshell.exe

and use the **tigericn.exe** file as the application icon.

Setup will also, by default, install the *ToolBook* runtime files and then attempt to create or modify the **asym.ini** file in the system's **Windows** directory, and attempt to modify **win.ini** by adding a line to the **[extensions]** section in order to associate **.tbk** files with the *ToolBook* executable. This can be avoided by foregoing installation of the *ToolBook* runtime (see Section 1.2 above).

After the Setup routine has finished, the files can be marked as Read Only access for .tbk files and Execute access for DLLs and executable files. This must be done in accordance with the Network Operating System manuals.

NB: By default the TransIt-TIGER Authoring Shell writes new 'books' (applications) created by the user to its own directory. The user can save to another location by prefixing the book name with the pathname of the new directory when prompted to save, and should be advised of this before using the Shell.

For further details regarding the operation of the *ToolBook* runtime, and how *TransIt-TIGER* uses previously-installed versions of *ToolBook*, please see the Technical Notes section at the end of this manual.

ACCESSING TRANSIT-TIGER AUTHORING SHELL ONCE IT HAS BEEN INSTALLED

NB: The design of the TransIt-TIGER Authoring Shell is such that you are not expected to have more than basic computing skills, that is the ability to operate a mouse and keyboard.

Double-click on the *TransIt-TIGER Authoring Shell* icon in Transit-TIGER Program Group: the TELL logo will appear, automatically followed after a short pause by the TransIt-TIGER **Title Screen**. At this point, you should press three keys simultaneously to gain access to the *TransIt-TIGER Shell* as an author: **Control**, **Shift** and **Right Arrow** Cursor. Then you will be prompted for a password: you should type in the password **leofric**. If the password is correctly entered, you will now see a Setup button in the lower left-hand part of the screen. Click on the **Setup** button and the Setup Screen will be presented, enabling you to begin authoring your application as follows.

Main title

Edit the text of the main title to show the title of your application. For example, in place of *Shell V 4.0.* you might want to enter *TransIt-TIGER Welsh.*

Character palette

If you wish a character palette to appear on screen to facilitate typing accented characters when entering or editing text in *TransIt-*

TIGER, edit the buttons as required and click on the **Enable Character Buttons** box so that it contains an X. For details on editing the character buttons, see Appendix A below.

External link

If you wish to enable the External Link facility, click on the **Select External Link** button. This calls up the Windows File Manager to enable you to select an appropriate .exe file. Click on the **Name Link** button to enter a caption for the External Link button from which you will call this external program (e.g. an on-line dictionary) when running *TransIt-TIGER* as a student. The external program would take over the screen until you exited from it again to return to *TransIt-TIGER* where you left off.

Set password

If you click on the **Set Password** button, you will be prompted to type in a new password of your choosing, to replace **leofric** as the password for entering this particular application (e.g. *TransIt-TIGER Welsh*) as an author in order to develop it further, edit it and so on. **Type in a password of not more than eight letters, taking care to remember it.**

When editing of the above is complete, exit **Setup** by pressing the button labelled **Click here to continue**. This brings you back to the **Title Screen**, which now reflects the changes you have made to the Main Title.

Now click on the large button marked **Click Here to Continue**. You will now be asked to provide a name for the book, that is, a name for your new application. Type in, for example, Welsh. The name must not consist of more than eight letters. The application will be saved in the *TransIt-TIGER Authoring Shell* directory as a *ToolBook* .exe file based on this name, e.g. **c:\ttshell\welsh.exe**. (The **.exe** extension will be added automatically to the name you provide.) If you want to save it to another location prefix the book name with the required path eg **c:\ttshell\work\welsh** or **a:\welsh**.

ENTERING DATA IN YOUR TRANSIT-TIGER APPLICATION

The *TransIt-TIGER Shell* is intended to be used for the creation of a set of up to ten translation assignments involving source texts typically occupying one side of A4 or less in printed form. If authors enter texts of considerably greater length than this, or if they introduce very extensive glossaries and Hints files, all functions may not work as expected, due to inherent restrictions in the underlying Asymetrix ToolBook software. The maximum number of links that can be made in Glossary or Hints for a particular Assignment is 250. It is advisable to work to much lower limits than this in practice.

Advice

It's good practice to hold as much text as possible in external text files and import it into the application, rather than typing it in directly. This guards against any corruption or damage to the application. It also allows you, and any colleagues working with you on the application, to edit the text using ordinary text editors and wordprocessors, so that only one person need have access to the application proper to incorporate text within it.

To proceed to build your application, click on the large button marked **Click Here to Continue**. At this point you are presented with two options: **Author** or **Student**. To proceed to the authoring environment, click on **Author**. Selecting **Student** mode enables you to test the application as a student would see it. This is not appropriate until you have entered some data, as shown below. You also have the option to return to **Setup** to make alterations or to **Exit** your application at this point, by clicking on the relevant button. If you have changed the password from the original **leofric**, be sure to remember the new password in order to access the application again later as an author.

When you click on the **Author** button, the current **Contents Screen** is displayed, where you can list the titles of up to ten translation assignments. By clicking on one of the buttons in the lower part of this screen, you may choose to set up a new assignment, to remove an existing assignment, to edit an existing assignment, to change the title of an existing assignment, to preview an existing assignment as a student would see it, to return to the previous screen or to quit the current *TransIt-TIGER* authoring application.

When you click on **Add an Assignment**, you are prompted to provide a name for the new assignment and to set it up, or cancel it if you change your mind. If you go ahead and set up the assignment, the following **Authoring Menu** choices are then presented:

Create/Edit the source text (type in, retrieve or edit a text to be translated.)

When you select this option, a field will be presented in which you can type your source text or edit a text previously entered. A plain ASCII text file can be imported by first clicking on the **Import Source Text** button and specifying the path name when prompted. Click on the **Done** button when finished - this will return you to the **Authoring Menu**: you should now click the **Save Your Work** button. The other buttons on the screen enable you to **Test Your Assignment** (simulating student mode), **Print Your Work, Return to the Menu** (i.e. the list of assignments) or **End this Session** (quit the *TransIt-TIGER Authoring Shell*).

Create /Edit the Glossary (type in, retrieve or edit the Glossary file.)

When you select this option, a field will be presented in which you can type your Glossary list or edit a Glossary previously entered. The Glossary file must be entered in the following format, to enable the program to recognise the beginning and end of an entry and the end of the Glossary file.

~headword
line 1 of data about headword
...
line n of data about headword

~next headword
line 1 of data about headword
...
line n of data about headword

that is, a tilde (~) marks the start of a new headword. **Do not leave a space** between the ~ and the first letter of the headword. **Do not leave a space** after the headword – make a hard return with the Enter key. If a link is not successfully made, check that there is no (invisible!) space after the headword in the Glossary file. The end of the Glossary file must also be marked by a ~ .

You can import text from a plain ASCII text file by first clicking on the **Import Glossary Text** button and specifying the path name when prompted. You can also copy text from a text editor such as Word for Windows and paste it into *TransIt-TIGER*, preserving accented characters and so on.

The **Build Glossary** button will build the Glossary automatically. The program searches your current source text for all instances of the headwords listed in your current Glossary file. It creates hyper-text links from these words or phrases in the source text to the relevant Glossary entry. The link will not be made unless the text string in the source text matches the Glossary headword **exactly**. If you only want a link to be made to one specific example of a head-word which occurs more than once in the text, you should ensure that the headword is unique by including a whole phrase.

If the results of the **Build Glossary** procedure are not as you wish, you can manually modify, add or remove links by clicking on the **Modify Links** button and following the instructions given. Clicking on the Check Glossary button will produce a report of any hotwords which are not linked to an entry in the Glossary file. When you run *TransIt-TIGER* in student mode, clicking on any hotwords which are not linked will produce an error message: **Cannot find...**

Click on the **Done** button when you have finished creating the Glossary – this will return you to the **Authoring Menu**. You should now click the **Save Your Work** button. The other buttons on the screen enable you to **Test Your Assignment** (simulating student mode), **Print Your Work, Return to the Menu** (i.e. the list of assignments) or **Quit TransIt TIGER** (quit the *TransIt-TIGER Authoring Shell* program).

Create/Edit the hints

(Type in, retrieve or edit the Hints file.) When you select this option, you can build in Hints (information about grammar, translation tips etc.) to complement the Glossary information. The procedure is the same as for Glossary building.

Create/Edit the Context Information

(Type in, retrieve or edit the text to appear in the Context Window.) This gives information about the translation task proposed for the current assignment. It may give other background information which helps to place the source text in a wider context for the guidance of the translator.

Create/Edit Translation Version A

(Type in, retrieve or edit the first suggested translation.) The field is presented on screen, so that you can enter the required text by following the same procedure as under previous headings.

Create/Edit Translation Version B

(Type in, retrieve or edit the second suggested translation.) The field is presented on screen, so that you can enter the required text by following the same procedure as under previous headings.

Set/Change Assignment Password

(When you click on this button, you will be prompted to type in a password for the current Assignment.) The password should be a word of up to eight alphabetical characters, with no spaces, lower case only. It is recommended that passwords be not excessively cryptic, but easy to remember, to spell and to pronounce, as it is merely some measure of control, rather than a high level of secrecy, that is usually required.

TO EXIT FROM *TRANSIT-TIGER AUTHORING SHELL* AT ANY TIME

From the **Contents Screen** or the **Title Screen**: click on the **Exit** button in the lower right-hand corner of the screen.

From an authoring procedure (Create/Edit the Source Text, Create/Edit the Glossary, etc.), click on the **Done** button in the lower right-hand corner of the screen. This will return you to the **Authoring Menu** Screen: click on the **Quit TransIt-TIGER** button at the bottom of the screen.

NB: Remember to click on the Save Your Work button and follow the Save procedure before exiting the program.

RUNNING YOUR *TRANSIT-TIGER* APPLICATION

The friendliest way for both you and your students to run the application you've created is to create a program icon for it in Windows Program Manager. To do this:

1 In Program Manager, open up the group into which you wish to place the *TransIt-TIGER* icon.
2 From the menu bar choose **File | New**.
3 In the following dialogue choose **Program Item**.
4 In the **Program Item Properties** dialogue fill in the first two fields as follows:

● **Description**: the caption you want to appear under the program icon
● **Command Line**: the pathname of your application file, eg c:\ttshell\welsh.exe*. Alternatively you can use the **Browse...** button to find the file.

* if the development version of ToolBook is on your system you should use the runtime executable mtb30run.exe to run your application. See Technical notes at the end of this manual.

The remaining two fields can be left empty.

5 If you want to use the *TransIt-TIGER* icon, choose **Change Icon...** and in the following dialogue either enter the pathname of the **tigericn.exe** file or use the **Browse** button to find it.

6 Press **OK**.

An icon should now appear on your desktop, which when double-clicked should start up your application. (Instructions as to how to create program icons can also be found in your Windows manual and Program Manager online Help.)

If you don't want to create a program icon for your application you can run it directly by either choosing **File|Run** from the Program Manager or File Manager menu bar and entering the application pathname, eg **c:\ttshell\welsh.exe**, or double-clicking the filename in the File Manager window.

EDITING YOUR *TRANSIT-TIGER* APPLICATION
• •

You can edit an application that you've previously created by running it (see previous section) and then entering Author mode by pressing Control, Shift and Right Arrow Cursor and entering the password (either **leofric** or one you previously specified).

*NB: Do not attempt to edit your application using the **TransIt-TIGER Authoring Shell**, by running the Shell and entering the application name when entering Author mode. This will result in the loss of all data in the application.*

Running your Application as a Student

You can test your application, to see how it would appear to students, either from the Authoring Menu by clicking on the button to Test Your Assignment, or by selecting Student mode rather than Author mode on start-up. If you are authoring with this Shell, you are probably familiar with the way the student's version works, but a reminder is given below:

SCREEN LAYOUT

The screen layout for each translation assignment is identical. On entry, the screen is divided into the following main areas.

- The (upper) **Source Text Window**, showing the text to be translated.
- The (lower) **Context Window,** presenting background information about the text, guidance on how you should approach the translation task, etc. This window will not appear if no context has been entered by the author for the given assignment.
- The (lower) **Translation Window**, where you can type your translation when you have dismissed the Context Window, by clicking on the Source Text button.

SCREEN ELEMENTS

Source Text window

When you enter the translation assignment, the upper half of the screen displays the Source Text window. You are able to scroll through the source text independently of the translation you type into the Translation window, but remember that you can also consult the text in printed form, and you should as a matter of course first read the complete text in the manual or as a printout before beginning your translation.

Context window

The Context window is where information is given about the source text and the translation task. The Context window appears automatically in the lower half of the screen every time you enter an assignment, and it can be removed by clicking on the **Source Text**, **Glossary** or **Hints** button. You can recall it by means of the **Context** button, and close it in order to proceed with your translation, by clicking on the **Source Text** button. The Context window will not appear unless some text has been entered in it by the author.

Translation window

The Translation window is effectively a blank page for your translation. For more information on typing in your translation, see the section of this document called: Typing and editing text.

Active buttons

The strip of active buttons on the right of the screen offers on-line assistance for your translation assignment.

Source Text	Click on this button to restore the display of the source text when you do not wish to see the green text identifying Glossary or Hints items.
Glossary	Click on this button to call Glossary lookup. The items in the text which are explained in the glossary appear in green and the banner above the

Source Text window changes to read **Glossary:<Assignment Name>** to show that Glossary lookup mode is activated. When the mouse pointer is over one of these words, the arrow changes to a pointing hand shape to indicate that there is further information about that word or phrase. When you click on green text the **Glossary Browser** window appears in the lower part of the screen, with the selected item appearing at the top of the list. You may then browse through the glossary information with the scroll bar. Clicking on another word shown in green brings that word to the top line of the **Glossary Browser** window. Both the green text and the **Glossary Browser** window are dismissed by clicking on the **Source Text** button.

Hints

Click on this button to call for guidance on grammatical or syntactic problems and particular translation difficulties. Those items in the text for which such guidance is specifically available are shown in green. When the mouse pointer is over one of these items, the arrow changes to a pointing hand shape to indicate that information is available about that item. When you click on green text the **Hints Browser** window appears in the lower part of the screen, with the selected item appearing at the top of the list. You may then browse through the hints with the scroll bar. Clicking on another word shown in green brings that word to the top line of the **Hints Browser** window. Both the green text and the **Hints Browser** window are dismissed by clicking on the **Source Text** button.

Context

Clicking on this button recalls the **Context** window, which gives initial guidance about the translation task proposed for the current assignment. Alternatively, it may give other background information which helps to place the source text in a wider context for the guidance of the translator.

To dismiss the Context Window click on the Source Text button, Glossary or Hints button. Neither the Context button nor the Context Window will appear unless some Context information has been entered by the author.

Version A

This button provides in the lower window one of two possible translations into English for your reference (a password, provided by your tutor at an appropriate time, is required to access it). You may compare this translation with your own version in the window above.

Version B

This button provides in the lower window a second possible translation into English for your reference (a password, provided by your tutor at an appropriate time, is required to access it). You may compare this translation with your own version in the window above.

Version A and B

This button provides, in a window, two possible translations into English for your reference (a password, provided by your tutor at an appropriate time, is required to access them). You may compare these two alternative translations with the source text. If this button does not appear on the screen, it means that the author has not provided a second version.

Save/Retrieve

This button enables you to save your translation. When you click here you are offered the choice of **Save**, **Retrieve** or **Cancel** and prompted to insert a disk in drive A. By default your work will be saved to this disk with a name based on the assignment title, but you may also save under another name (to avoid overwriting previous work) and/or to another drive/directory.

Print

This button provides you with options either to send your translation immediately to the printer or to save your work to disk first and then to print. You can also print out the source text and versions

A and B, subject to permission via a password. The **Cancel** option enables you to return to the translation assignment and continue working before you print.

External link

This button gives access to an external program, such as an online dictionary or other reference source. The name of the external program available, if any, will be shown as the button's caption. If no external link is available, this button will not appear on the screen.

Go Back

This button takes you out of the translation assignment, back to the **Contents** screen.

Exit

Click on this button (on the **Contents** screen) to leave the *TransIt-TIGER* program.

TYPING AND EDITING TEXT

When you enter a new translation assignment, after you have dismissed the **Context** window the cursor is blinking in the top left hand corner of the translation window, ready for you to type in your translation. If the character palette is activated, you can click on the character buttons to enter accented characters into your text. This has the same effect as holding down the ALT key and typing in a code from the numerical keypad (see Appendix A).

Formatting your text

You may wish to type and print your text with the default settings. However, you are able to change the style and the size of the font (typescript) or underline or italicise certain terms or headings in your translation, using the Windows **Text** menu. To do this, you first need to highlight the text you wish to change before selecting different fonts, etc. (see Editing text below).

Highlighting text

Position the mouse pointer at the start of the word you wish to highlight. Press and hold down the left mouse button and move or 'drag' the mouse gently to the right. The text you highlight with the drag is put in inverse mode, i.e. blue letters on a black background. Release the mouse button when you have covered all the text you wish to highlight. Note that the highlighting is removed if you click again anywhere in that text window.

Editing text

Below the bar at the top of the screen is a white bar containing two menu headings: **Edit** and **Text**. These are the menus to help you edit the format of your translation. Note that only options which are visible in heavy black type can be implemented, not those in pale grey. To implement any of the options, you can either click on the menu item or use the keyboard shortcut given alongside the item.

Edit

Note that **Edit** will work only on pre-defined text. If you have not highlighted any text, then the first four options will be visible in pale grey and will not function.

The **Edit** menu contains the following options:

- **Undo**: undoes the very last typing you have done
- **Cut**: removes the highlighted text to temporary storage
- **Copy**: creates a copy of the highlighted text in temporary storage
- **Paste**: retrieves whatever was last placed in temporary storage and 'pastes' it at the point where the cursor is positioned in the text
- **Clear**: removes the highlighted text permanently
- **Select all**: highlights all of the text.

Text

Note that the **Text** options will work only on pre-defined text. If you have not highlighted any text, then the changes will only apply to text you add from that point on.

The **Text** menu contains the following options:

Character... leads to a selection window by which you may alter the appearance of your text:

- **Style**: bold, underline, italic or strikeout
- **Font**: a wide selection of character fonts
- **Point size**: a selection of character sizes available for the selected font
- **Apply**: shows what the text would look like if the changes you select are applied
- **OK**: accepts and processes any changes.
- **Cancel**: takes you back to the text, without making any changes

Paragraph... leads to a selection window by which you may alter the layout of your text:

- **Alignment** (of margins): left, right, centre or justify
- **Spacing**: single, 1½ or double
- **Tab type**: left tabs or decimal tabs
- **Tab spacing**: the default setting can be altered if required
- **Indents from edge of field**: the default settings can be altered if required
- **Apply**: shows what the text would look like if the changes you select are applied
- **OK**: accepts and processes any changes
- **Cancel**: takes you back to the text without making any changes.

Regular puts the text in plain unformatted print.
Bold puts the text in bold print.
Italic puts the text in italics.
Underline underlines the text.
Strikeout draws a horizontal line through the whole text (to cross out mistakes perhaps?).

Technical Notes

DEVELOPMENT VERSION OF *TOOLBOOK* INSTALLED ON THE SYSTEM

If you have the full development version of *ToolBook* on your system you need to be aware of the following two potential problems regarding the installation and running of *TransIt-TIGER*.

1 During installation the Setup program looks for the **asym.ini** file in the **\Windows** directory, and if it exists reads the **[Registered Apps]** section to determine the default installation directory. This will contain the pathname of the full version of *ToolBook* so if you leave the default installation path unchanged Setup may overwrite important files in your *ToolBook* directory and will make alterations to **asym.ini**.

2 *TransIt-TIGER* has been packaged as an .exe file using the **Save As .EXE** menu option in the *ToolBook* **File** menu. When this 'executable' is run it looks at the **[ToolBook Load Information]** section in **asym.ini** to find the main *ToolBook* executable with which to run *TransIt-TIGER* and will thus use the development version of *ToolBook*.

Problem 1 can be avoided by either not installing the *ToolBook* runtime during Setup (if you have version 3.0a of *ToolBook* installed) or by instructing Setup to install it elsewhere than your *ToolBook* directory (see Sections 1.1 and 1.2 of Installing *TransIt-TIGER*).

Whilst problem 2 is not serious, insofar as a password is required to enter Author mode, it may result in slower application execution than if the runtime engine were used. To remedy this you need to slightly alter the command line in the Program Item Properties of the *TransIt-TIGER* icon to read:

<runtime dir.>\mtb30run.exe *<application dir.>*\tshell.exe

(If you have *Multimedia ToolBook 3.0a* installed *<runtime dir.>* can be your ToolBook directory, as this contains all the necessary runtime files.)

TOOLBOOK RUNTIME INSTALLATION

TransIt-TIGER comes with the runtime modules from *Asymetrix Multimedia ToolBook version 3.0a*. Unless specifically instructed otherwise (see Installing *TransIt-TIGER*, Sections 1.1 and 1.2) the application Setup routine will install the runtime files in the default directory. **Any existing ToolBook files in the directory will be overwritten without warning**. This will result in problems if you are running applications developed in earlier versions of ToolBook, and so it is advisable to check the timestamps of the files in the *ToolBook* runtime directory **before** installing *TransIt-TIGER* and take the appropriate action (see table below).

Timestamp	ToolBook version	Action
01:53 or earlier	1.53 or earlier	Install the *TransIt-TIGER* runtime in a different directory (see Installing *TransIt-TIGER*, Section 1.1).
03:00	3.0	Overwrite this version with the *TransIt-TIGER* runtime.
03:01	3.0a	No need to install *TransIt-TIGER* runtime (see Installing *TransIt-TIGER*, Section 1.2).
04:00 or later	4.0 or later	Install the *TransIt-TIGER* runtime in a different directory (see Installing TransIt-TIGER, Section 1.1).

Appendix A:
Accented Characters

To set up a character button in **Setup** (Author Mode), click on it and at the prompt enter the data as follows:

Hold down the **Alt** key, while typing the relevant code from the numerical keypad,

e.g. for ä **Alt 132**. The character will appear when you have completed the code and released the **Alt** key. After the character, type = and the code, e.g. ä =132. To confirm, click **ok**.

The following are the codes for the most common accented characters. For other characters, consult the relevant table of characters in your DOS manual.

French	German	Italian	Spanish
à = 133	ä = 132	à = 133	á = 160
â = 131	Ä = 142	è = 138	é = 130
é = 130	ö = 148	ì = 141	í = 161
É = 144	Ö = 153	ò = 149	ó = 162
è = 138	ü = 129	ù = 151	ú = 163
ê = 136	Ü = 154		ñ = 164
î = 140	ß = 225		¿ = 168
ï = 139			
ô = 147			
ç = 135			
Ç = 128			

Appendix B:
Basic principles of the Windows environment

The *Translt-TIGER Authoring Shell* is a Windows application and uses the standard functions and keys of any Windows application. Below are a few basic principles with which you are advised to become familiar before running *Translt-TIGER Authoring Shell*.

- **Single clicks on the mouse are all you need for the majority of tasks.**
  For this, you position the mouse pointer (usually an arrow shape) over the desired item on the screen and depress the button on the left-hand side of your mouse once. It is important to allow time for the computer to respond to your actions and not to click repeatedly on the item if you have already clicked once.

- **Double-clicks on the mouse are needed for a few selected functions and in order to start running a program in Windows.**
  For this, you position the mouse pointer over the item and depress the left-hand button of your mouse twice in rapid succession. As with single clicks, it is important to allow time for the computer to respond before trying to click again.

- **Various options are available through pull-down menus.**
  The menus are displayed by clicking on one of the menu headings (**Edit** or **Text**) in the bar along the top of the screen. Only those options which are visible in heavy black type may be

selected, not those in pale grey. Please note that most changes only affect text which has been selected.

- **In TransIt-TIGER (Student Mode), the Translation Window is the only one in which you can type**

- **Scrolling through text.**
  If a window contains more text than is currently visible, a "scroll bar" appears on the right of the text area. A scroll bar is a vertical strip with an arrow at each end, the one at the top pointing up and the one at the bottom pointing down. There is a silver indicator box in the scroll bar which gives you an indication of your position in the text. You can move your view of the text up and down by means of the up or down arrows. Note that this changes only your view of the text, not the text itself.

- **You may exit the system at any time.**
  Click on the button marked **Exit** at the bottom right-hand corner of the screen or double-click on the small silver box in the top left-hand corner of the screen.

  The system may then ask if you want to save any changes. Click on the **No** option. This does not affect any translation assignments a student has saved to floppy disk during a work session.